YOUR KNOWLEDGE HAS VA

Bibliographic information published by the German National Library:

The German National Library lists this publication in the National Bibliography; detailed bibliographic data are available on the Internet at http://dnb.dnb.de .

Imprint:

Copyright © 2017 GRIN Verlag, Open Publishing GmbH
Print and binding: Books on Demand GmbH, Norderstedt Germany
ISBN: 9783668412552

This book at GRIN:

http://www.grin.com/en/e-book/355110/distributed-agile-outsourcing-an-overview-of-methods-and-success-factors

Oliver Götz

Distributed Agile Outsourcing. An Overview of Methods and Success Factors

GRIN Publishing

GRIN - Your knowledge has value

Since its foundation in 1998, GRIN has specialized in publishing academic texts by students, college teachers and other academics as e-book and printed book. The website www.grin.com is an ideal platform for presenting term papers, final papers, scientific essays, dissertations and specialist books.

Oliver Götz

Distributed Agile Outsourcing. An Overview of Methods and Success Factors

GRIN Publishing

GRIN - Your knowledge has value

Since its foundation in 1998, GRIN has specialized in publishing academic texts by students, college teachers and other academics as e-book and printed book. The website www.grin.com is an ideal platform for presenting term papers, final papers, scientific essays, dissertations and specialist books.

Visit us on the internet:

http://www.grin.com/

http://www.facebook.com/grincom

http://www.twitter.com/grin_com

Distributed Agile Outsourcing - an Overview of Methods and Success Factors

Oliver Götz

Abstract

IT outsourcing (ITO) engagements have become one of the prevailing IT strategies. Moreover, agile software development (ASD) approaches tend to replace traditional, sequential methods. Injecting ASD into ITO leads to agile global or distributed outsourced development (AGOSD/ADOSD) projects characterized by using agile methods within distributed environments rising the challenge of facilitating coordination and collaboration between teams. Especially, communication between client and external vendor became one of the major critical success factors. Consequently, my study examines communication practices within global IT projects. (1) I conducted a structured literature review to extend the list of communication practices provided by prior studies. (2) I consolidated and categorized them. (3) By having performed expert interviews, I deployed a ranking pointing out their practical relevance.

1

Contents

1. Introduction

Within the past ten years, the question about "make or buy" has a recognizable trend on the buy-side in the Information Technology (IT) sector, since organizations increasingly spend funds on Information Technology Outsourcing (ITO) projects [11]. According to conservative estimates, in 2010, the amount for expenses in global ITO exceeded 270$ billion underlying the fact that the introductory question is permanently on the agenda of management decisions [27]. In global outsourced software development projects, stakeholders from various time zones, organizational and national cultures are involved in the process [4]. Tasks at different stages of the software lifecycle can be segregated and implemented at multiple geographies coordinated by applying communication and information technologies [18]. ITO comprises business benefits such as the proximity to market, the utilization of market opportunities quickly building cross-national, virtual teams and the possibility to work in different time zones. Hence, it enables the development of software "round-the-clock" [28, 25, 18].

In parallel to the rise of ITO, agile software development (ASD) methods revealed a success-promising approach for organizations [10] since it addresses the key problems in traditional software development, such as too long development cycles, high costs and the product's defectiveness [1, 13, 4]. Instead, it enables simplicity and speed, puts focus on individuals, customer collaboration, interactions and quick response to changes [8, 6]. Furthermore, according to the Standish Group 2015 Chaos Report [7], 39% of 50.000 software development projects measured between 2011 and 2015, applying agile methods, were successful. In contrast, 11% projects with a waterfall development environment succeeded. Looking at the size of the projects, from tiny enhancements until big re-engineering implementations, only 3% of the large projects using a waterfall model achieved their goal, whereas 19% following an agile approach were favorable [7].

Combining ITO and ASD leads to the term "agile global outsourced software development" (AGOSD) and "agile distributed outsourced software development" (ADOSD), which are considered as synonyms. The core of AGOSD projects is, that client organizations outsource software development projects to external vendors, near- and offshore [22]. The vendors apply agile development methods such as Scrum or Exreme Programming (XP) within virtual teams. Teams usually consist of members from all around the world working together on that project [24, 25]. Dreesen et. al [5] and Schmidt and Meures [20] have already coped with AGOSD by identifying communication practices and empirically examined them. Schmidt and Meures [20] ranked them concerning their practical relevance by conducting a

3

survey and questionnaire. Yet, there are no reasons available why a communication practice got this rank. So deeper knowledge about its practical meaning is missing. Hence, I define the following research question, guiding my research endeavor: *"How important are the current known communication practices in AGOSD with regards to large IT projects, why are these important and which ones are missing?"*

The remainder of the paper is structured as follows. The next section provides information on the theoretical background, mainly on the related work this paper is built upon and specifically on the terminology ASD and AGOSD respectively ADOSD. In the third section, I will outline my research design including the research process, data collection and analysis. In the fourth section, I will describe my findings. In the fifth section, I will discuss the research results by giving not only theoretical but also practical implications. Additionally, I will show up the limitations of my research project as well as suggest future research directions to extend our knowledge about AGOSD. Lastly, I will wrap up the paper with a conclusion.

2. Theoretical Background

2.1 Related Work

My research project mainly builds upon the research papers by [5] and [20]. Dreesen et al. [5] performed a structured literature review on both communication practices in ASD and AGOSD. As a result, they identified 42 communication practices within agile projects, 23 of them are dedicated for AGOSD not being applicable for ASD without a further specification.

Schmidt and Meures [20] research consisted of a structured literature review and of the empirical examination of agile communication practices. They made use of interviews to derive new ones and questionnaires to rank them in order to determine their practical relevance. To sum up, they identified 42 communication practices which are congruent with the results from Dreesen et al. [5]. Furthermore, within the scope of the empirical part, they identified 5 additional practices.

With agile development projects being on the rise [19, 24], Passivaara, Durasiewicz and Lassenius [16] developed a framework of supporting practices for global software development comprising five distinct categories. These categories enable to classify the identified communication practices. Taking into account the upcoming challenges from distributed agile development, the first category is *frequent visits* for generating and fostering trust as well as improving collaboration. The second one is *multiple communication modes,* describing the parallel application of different communication methods. Third category is *mirroring / balanced sites*, containing dependency reducing practices. The next category is *ambassador / rotating guru*, including methods for the implementation of expert roles and the last one is *synchronization of work hours*, incorporating practices to maximize overlapping work hours.

2.2 AGOSD – A symbiosis of ITO and ASD

The outsourcing of software development is the shift of special services to an external vendor [12, 21]. With Internet-based collaboration services and the increasing engagement with providers located in Latin America, China and India for software development services [12, 3], a huge ration of the outsourced software development projects is furnished by virtual teams [2], where team members are located in different geographies and work together in common manner. On the one hand, this leads to cost reduction potential and smoothens the way for further business opportunities [3, 28]. On the other hand, it generates additional challenges such as adapted control and coordination mechanisms, technology and the integration of people coming from different geographies, cultural backgrounds and working [28, 25].

Agile software development aims to enable faster response times to changing customer requirements as well as an acceleration of development cycles [23] and hence, it follows an iterative approach which is quite the contrary to waterfall or sequential approaches [15]. This leads to continuous communication and interactions between the vendor respectively developer team and the client, so that the client is directly involved in the software development process [23]. In addition, agile processes improve team moral, i. e. it is told what to deliver but not how, overall quality and efficiency, since each iteration (sprint) ends with a testing phase [15]. To a large extent, present-day organizations implement agile development methods in general and especially for global distributed development projects much more frequently [9].

The combination of ITO and ASD results in AGOSD. It has been pointed out, that communication between client and external provider is one of the most critical success factor an AGOSD engagement has to cope with [14, 9, 15].

5

3. Research Method

3.1 Data Collection

My data collection consisted of three consecutive steps which are depicted in Figure 1:

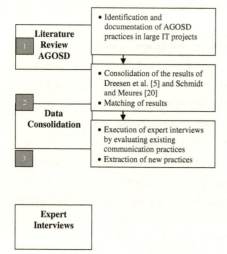

Figure 1: Analysis Approach

(1) I conducted a structured literature review on the basis of the recommendation by Webster and Watson [26]. The review started with a keyword search on communication practices within AGOSD projects in particular, followed by a backward and forward search. I defined a search string (table 1) for the keyword search to identify relevant articles in databases (ProQuest, EBSCOhost, INFORMS).

Table 1: Search String

Field	Search String
Communication practices and success factors in AGOSD	(agil* OR scrum OR extreme programming OR xp) AND (distribut* OR outsourc* OR offshor* OR global) AND development* AND (communication OR success factors)

There was no restriction for the publishing year of the articles. To ensure high quality, I only filtered peer reviewed articles. All search results were examined regarding title, abstract, and keywords. In total, my final set of articles consisted of 23 articles.

(2) I consolidated the results from Dreesen et al. [5] and Schmidt and Meures [20] by matching the found dedicated AGOSD communication practices with the corresponding categories suggested by the framework of Paasivaara, Durasiewicz and Lassenius [17].

(3) Based on step (2), I created an interview guideline. After that, I conducted two expert interviews to gain insights of the importance of communication practices in ADOSD in large IT projects. Table 2 shows an overview of the participants. Both of them have been working or are currently engaged within a distributed agile environment.

Table 2: Overview of participants

NO	ROLE	EXP
1	Technical and Team Lead	3,5
2	Delivery Manager	1
Legend: Role = Official job description of the participant; EXP = Years of experience in this specific role		

The interviewees allowed to record the interview. I used Skype to process the interview and thus, I could use Callnote, a recording software for online phone calls ensuring high audio quality. Correlating the interview insights to the research question, I made clear in the beginning that they should position themselves in a member within a distributed agile outsourced team developing a large software package such as an enterprise system. For each practice I asked the interviewees how they would rate it on a Likert Scale, i.e. 5 very important and 1 less important. I wrapped up the interview with questions regarding the interviewee's opinion about distributed agile outsourced software development, if a communication practice is missing and an overall statement, if a pure AGOSD is suitable for large projects.

3.2 Data Analysis

After the data collection phase, I performed a thorough analysis of the gathered data from the literature review, the results of Dreesen et al. [5] and Schmidt and Meures [20] as well as from the interviews.

7

Since both interview partners agreed about recording them, I transcribed the interviews with Express Scribe. Hence, I was able to provide representative quotes to justify why the interviewee has rated the communication practice with the appropriate number of the Likert Scale. After having transcribed all interviews, I gathered all rates in a table. The implementation of the 5-point Likert Scale enabled me to do a ranking and to identify which communication practice suits best to distributed agile outsourced large projects. If an interviewee mentioned a method or practice which has not been listed in the pool of agile communication practices yet, I added it to the corresponding category and formatted it with an italic style. In this case no ranking was feasible because it is a newly-found practice and I conducted the interviews within a narrow timeframe.

4. Results

4.1 AGOSD communication practices for large IT projects in the literature

After having conduced the structured literature review, to the best of my knowledge and understanding, I could not find any new dedicated communication practice in AGOSD for large IT projects that has not been listed by Dreesen et al. [5] and Schmidt and Meures [20] yet.

4.2 Overview of AGOSD communication practices in large projects

After the data consolidation, I was able to create table 3 showing an overall summary of current, dedicated AGOSD communication practices. For completeness, I also added the newly-found practice derived from the interview analysis for simplified readability and hence, it can fulfill the purpose of a reference manual. I performed a profound analysis of the rank and its justification in the upcoming section by providing representative quotes of the interviewees.

Table 3: Overview of AGOSD communication practices in large IT projects

ID	DESCRIPTION	R	M	I#1	I#2
1. Category: Frequent Visits					
1.1	Establishing team member trust	1	5	5	5
1.2	Rotation of employees	2	2,5	3	2
2. Category: Multiple Communication Modes					
2.1	Groupware tools and other collaboration technologies (e. g. Jira, Lync)	1	5	5	5
2.2	IT infrastructure (high-speed data connection)	2	4,5	5	4
2.3	Development of a project-specific communication methodology	2	4,5	5	4
2.4	Stakeholder analysis	4	4	4	4
2.5	Project Management Systems	5	3	2	4
2.6	Social networking	5	3	3	3
ID	DESCRIPTION	R	M	I#1	I#2
2.7	Use as many communication channels as possible	7	2,5	3	2
3. Category: Mirroring / Balanced Sites					
3.1	Improvement of cooperation	1	5	5	5
3.2	„One Team" – mentality	1	5	5	5
3.3	Trainings (language, communication, technology and intercultural training)	3	4,5	5	4
3.4	Community of Practice (know-how deepening)	4	3,5	4	3
3.5	Similar team compositions at various locations	5	3	3	3
3.6	Avoidance of communication loops	5	3	2	4
3.7	Clarifying general questions in advance of meeting	5	3	2	4
3.8	*"Lessons-Learned" - sessions*	-	-	-	-

9

4. Category: Ambassador / Rotating Guru					
4.1	Creation of a joint knowledge base	1	5	5	5
4.2	Expert / mediator rotation	2	4,5	4	5
5. Category: Synchronization of Work Hours					
5.1	Improved documentation (incremental, if necessary and time saving)	1	4,5	4	5
5.2	Provide project-specific guidelines/standards (behavior, communication)	1	4,5	4	5
5.3	Explicit targets (define milestones)	1	4,5	5	4
5.4	Generating a compatible ICT and media convergence	1	4,5	5	4
5.5	Synchronization of Work Hours	5	4	4	4

Legend: ID = ID of the communication practices enabling easy reference, practices in *italic* illustrate a method derived from the interviews; DESCRIPTION = Brief description of the method; R = Rank for the method's practical relevance resulting from the mean; M = Arithmetic mean of the rates computed by the two interviewees provided rates; IV #[Number] = Interviewee who assed each communication practice with a number (usage of a 5-point Likert Scale: 5 = very important / 1 = less important)

4.3 Practical relevance of dedicated AGOSD communication practices in large projects

4.3.1. Category 1: Frequent Visits. This category contains practices to improve the inter-team relationship. *Establishing team member trust* seems to be the most important factor in this category. Both interviewees rated it with a 5:

"You know, it is the most important thing [...] What I noticed when I was working with foreign people, every person comes from a different cultural mindset [...] [Trust] smoothens all and the project actually. I have also noticed what happens when the trust factor is partly missing: the person who is assigning the work to another team member in an another

geography feels the need to constantly check the progress on it and ask for hourly reports". (Interviewee 1, 66-82)

As interviewee 1 mentioned, trust is attributed an enormous level of importance, especially while working across different geographies. The statement of interviewee 2 is in alignment with the declaration of interviewee 1. Moreover, he underlined the quality of assigned tasks, i.e. people have to fulfill trust by delivering results with high quality.

Looking at *rotation of employees*, the interviewees assigned a lower rate. According to interviewee 1, it does not make any difference in relation to the performance of the agile team:

"With my project experience what I can say is, I have been in a project where people were doing a rotation as well as you said. People who were working as developers on the Java front, there would be a loss when they work on the database front [...] I could see it helped. I could also see in another project where there was no such kind of rotation policy and that worked as well like the other one. I could not see any additional benefit." (Interviewee 1, 88-93)

4.3.2 Category 2: Multiple Communication Modes. The category *multiple communication modes* comprises the usage of several communication channels respectively modes within distributed agile outsourced projects. It consists of seven different communication practices.

Both interviewees have clearly pointed out the necessity of special *groupware tools and collaboration technologies*, since it enables quick information sharing "rather than going in emails and things like that [...] and you could give access to all these people" (Interviewee 1, 126-130). Moreover, this practice improves the effectiveness within team communication and facilitates the inter-team collaboration (Interviewee 2).

On the second rank, there is the *IT infrastructure*. It is an essential factor that the productivity within a team is guaranteed:

"This again comes from personal experience because we had a project which was basically on JBOS middleware system. One of the major problems for us was the following: we constantly used to [encounter] memory issues because the laptops which we were using had just eight gigabyte of RAM and we needed to upgrade it to 16 gigabyte. I could see dramatically how the productivity of each team member increased as soon as we got our new laptops. I mean basically the RAM upgrades. I would say this is probably the most important thing." (Interviewee 1, 152-158)

11

Furthermore, interviewee 2 (translated from German, 1. 83-84) put emphasis on the satisfaction within teams, especially referring to developers since "the developers' satisfaction suffers, if the connection is slow [and the hardware is poor]".

On the same level of importance is the *development of a project-specific communication methodology*. This is required because standard communication methods, such as emails, tend to have an overflow. In addition, verbal and face-to-face communication enhance the understanding and results can be shown live, as well as discussed:

"We used to have [a project-specific methodology] in our agile project, we used to have something like a team [meeting] where it is used to go to a location and have a quick discussion where each team member could explain what he has done the day before, what he is doing today and what he plans to do the day after. The reason why this was so important is simple: this approach enabled the team lead to understand quickly where we were and where team members needed help, where colleagues needed support and deliverables were lacking behind some priority queues. So I would say this is very important because email tends to accumulate, it tends to be sometimes more distracting rather than achieving the purpose." (Interviewee 1, 185-192)

From a Scrum perspective, interviewee 2 also emphasized the face-to-face communication (Sprint planning with screen-sharing) as indispensable to enhance the effectiveness.

Stakeholder analysis is ranked on the fourth position and both interviewees gave to this indicator the same degree of importance. On the one hand, including stakeholders helps to prevent miscommunication because

"I see within a [distributed] agile project the most important benefit it brings is, the amount of communication which goes through. People implicitly get to know what is required by them [...]" (Interviewee 1, 175-179)

On the other hand, each team member knows who is involved in the project in order "to understand and properly prioritize [tasks]" (Interviewee 2, translated from German, 101-102), e.g. tasks from the product owner need to have a priority in contrast to ones coming from a team member that are not critical for fulfilling a milestone.

Project management systems and *social networking* share the fifth rank. At first, I consider *project management systems*. Interviewee 1 (137-142) rated it with a 2, as he argued that

"for one of my projects we had nothing more than an Excel sheet. We just marked down the tasks which we had and as a team lead, I would just use an Excel sheet to track what people are doing. So of course, if I use Microsoft Project or similar programs, it would probably be

a little bit more helpful, but I do not see this a major factor to run an agile project. I could see that we could run it pretty well."

In contrast, interviewee 2 (translated from German, 75-77) highlighted the importance of such kind of tools since it is a fundamental part of a scrum methodology implementation, so that the "Scrum Master knows, in what direction the current development advances and the committed scope can be finished at the end".

Social Networking is not essential for an agile project's success rather than it comprises a couple of misfits. The challenge is that having mobile devices and push notifications activated as well as regular account synchronization, it is not possible to avoid an app's power of instant messaging, even in the leisure time:

"The only issue is that people do not know when to draw a line and when to stop sending requests within social networking. Nowadays, everybody uses a mobile phone; [...] even when you are logged off work, you would still have your mobile phone. The problem is any request coming across social networking you would still get it and when you are at your personal space, you just do not want to be interrupted with work related stuff." (Interviewee 1, 163-169)

Very little importance has been attributed to the indicator *use as many communication channels as possible.* Interviewee 1 claimed that as long as it is within business hours, there is no argument against a high quantity of communication methods. However, social network technologies such as WhatsApp penetrate into the business environment and establish a new communication culture. Consequently, requests are posted and this implicitly serves the purpose, that this task has to be finished as soon as possible, especially when a manager creates tasks:

"I experienced in another one of my projects what used to happen when people created a WhatsApp group. Since we worked in different geographies and different times zones we got requests on WhatsApp even if the business hours had been finished. This behavior built up a very weird culture: it was 8 or 9 pm and I would get a request on my WhatsApp asking me 'Can you please do this' even though of course I would say it would not be like... they are forcing me to do something like that, then there would be a kind of pressure on me how to do it. Of course, since I was little bit seemed, I could not straight away say it is not possible. I would be looking at it tomorrow, of course depending on the urgency. But I could see my team members who were probably lower down in the hierarchy had a little bit difficulties in saying No to these kind of requests actually." (Interviewee 1, 110-119)

13

Additionally, if there is no addressee explicitly mentioned, the task could be forgotten in the mass of WhatsApp messages. Building upon this, instead of raising the quantity of communication channels, more effort should be put into the increase of a channel's effectiveness, such as high quality video conference (Interviewee 2).

4.3.3 Category 3: Mirroring / Balances Sites. This category comprises practices to reduce dependencies or to soften up interdependencies between sites.

Improvement of cooperation and *"One Team" – mentality* are both on the top rank since the interviewees rated it with a 5. A bad cooperation within and between teams significantly decreases the productivity due to a poor communication and wrong assignment of tasks:

"The reason is that I have come across instances in teams which I was leading where the communication between teams sometimes tended to be poor and sometimes hostile. The reason for that could be anything. The database teams failed because this job is not supposed to be done by them, but it should have been executed by the development team. As a consequence, the development team failed because it should be the database team who should be doing it and facts like these. This led to bad mood between teams and it does not help in doing anything where small things get escalated quickly. So I would say that cooperation definitely helps." (Interviewee 1, 253-260)

However, these practices profit each other by synergy effects. A good *cooperation* may improve to build a *"One Team" – mentality* as "I would link up this with the cooperation point" (Interviewee 1, 265-266). Everybody should feel involved in the project and get the feeling that he partially contributes to the project' success, resulting in a high motivation (Interviewee 2).

Trainings, such as language, communication, technology and inter-cultural training, are also an important factor to balance sites and reduce dependencies. For instance, language barriers have to be mitigated to improve collaboration:

"I have seen across other geographies as well, there tends to be a problem where people are unable to communicate in English and unfortunately, when I am working from an Indian perspective, English is probably the main language [...] So probably some kind of training on the client which could be e. g. French, German or Spanish. would probably help the understanding." (Interviewee 1, 225-238)

Furthermore, trainings are important for the team's development. On the one hand, the team members are able to set their professional skills on the next level. On the other hand, inter cultural training, i.e. getting knowledge about religion and traditions, contributes to a better understanding of the team members' behavior coming from different geographies (Interviewee 2).

Community of practice is on rank 4. Following the statement of interviewee 1 (293-294), "it basically helps people not to reinvent a wheel or spending time how to do that", since recurring issues can be easily avoided if they have been discussed in an expert meeting before. Interviewee 2 mentioned so called Brownbag-Sessions where topics are introduced that might be interesting for the future. However, both of the interview partners rated it less important.

The fifth place is shared by *(1) similar team compositions at various locations, (2) avoidance of communication loops* and *(3) clarifying general questions in advance of meeting.*

As to (1) there is no significant finding in the interviews that this practice does contribute to an agile project's success, nor put some constraints on the team's performance.

There is a similar reason for (2), since, for instance double sending a message, does not influence the outcome (Interviewee 1). However, interviewee 2 (148-149) argued that it is useful "to include responsible persons in the very beginning, so that they can contribute to a solution early enough [although having redundancy then]." So this practice has important components if it is purposefully applied at the right time.

Interviewee 1 stated, that (3) is not critical for a project's success as these kind of questions such as layout of progress reports, contact persons crystalize after a couple of meetings. There is no need to spend time on clarifying this at the beginning. Yet, according to interviewee 2, each participation in a meeting should be prepared well enough in order to fulfill the agenda's content. The level of detail of the meeting preparation depends on the meeting owner. For instance, if a customer is joining the meeting, the meeting is supposed to be perfectly prepared and organized.

Finally, interviewee 2 mentioned *"Lessons-Learned" – sessions,* which is a new one communication practice, after each iteration or sprint cycle has been finished. It is useful to have "a sprint retrospective, always looking at aspects which could be improved [for the next time]" (Interviewee 2, 221-222).

4.3.4 Category 4: Ambassador / Rotating Guru. This category comprises practices for the implementation of expert roles/knowledge.

Interviewee 1 and 2 both highly assessed the *creation of a joint knowledge base*. On the one hand, "a good knowledge database would be very helpful because it would facilitate the awareness of the functionalities of the system by all other team members" (Interviewee 1, 329-330) and will enable to wipe out deficiencies, e.g. how the system works, what are the involved entities etc. On the other hand, "coding guidelines are supposed to be written down to avert the repetition of mistakes" (Interviewee 2, 196-170).

Expert/mediator rotation is at the second place. Interviewee 1 (337-338) shed light on the importance of "a facilitator or mediator, who acts as a technical expert for specific teams". He is the one, who is responsible for harmony in the team, "strengthens the cohesion within a team" (Interviewee 2, translated from German, 176-177) and helps to solve problems, because "when you have a challenge, it is preferable to have the issue fixed as soon as possible rather than waiting for the next day or week" (Interview 1, 342-345).

4.3.5 Category 5: Synchronization of Work Hours. This category consists of practices that maximize the overlapped work hours between distributed agile teams. *(1) Improved documentation, (2) provide project-specific guidelines/standards (behavior, communication), (3) explicit targets (define milestones)* and *(4) generating a compatible ICT and media convergence* are practices being equally ranked on position one.

(1) is attributed a high importance regarding fluctuation within a company:

"What generally happens is, there are people who would leave the project or leave the company; this leads to new team members joining the project who would probably not have good idea about the application and what it is designed with, how it works and different functionalities of it." (Interviewee 1, 366-372)

Looking at the statements for (2), both interviewees argued that, regarding compliance issues, it is quite important to have stringent guidelines. These enable to reduce to frivolous handling with organization-specific data because "I have seen cases where people would be sharing across passwords, multiple people mailed me emails etc." (Interviewee 1, 381-382).

(3) also received a high rate from both interviewees. Interviewee 2 (translated from German, l. 203-205) drew a causal relationship between effectiveness and goal definition as he clarified that "if you work towards a specific goal, you work also more effectively, i.e. if you have prioritized your tasks." This result is enhanced in account of setting a kind of pressure on the employees:

"I had another project where there was actually no specific milestone set and what tended to happen was people would get a little bit more relaxed [...] the same problem would be applicable to an agile project [...] If you do not have a milestone and you do not know what you are trying to achieve or what is your target, [the team acts blindly]. So this would be very important, so that the team is oriented to a single goal rather where people think we can take it relaxed, we can do it when it becomes necessary." (Interviewee 1, 387-394)

An agile project's outcome is doomed to fail, unless used technologies, that are going to be implemented for collaboration, are aligned between the distributed teams. Interview partner 1 (399-402) postulated (4) as "a prerequisite [...] whenever a project is being configured, it has to be mentioned [which technologies have to be used]" since it builds the core of distributed collaboration.

On the fifth place lies *synchronization of work hours*. Each of the interviewees rated it with a 4. Without a doubt, the fact of having overlapping work hours is necessary in an agile environment, especially for daily scrums, in order to evaluate the sprint status. Additionally, delivery times have to be ensured for reducing the loss of data and delays (Interviewee 2). Furthermore, synchronized work hours positively affect the work-life balance, since no requests are sent outside of business times (Interviewee 1). Even more so, this practice mitigates misunderstandings and accelerates response times:

"It is a lot easier then to get clarifications because they can be done in a real time basis where we could have a call which is within the work times in both countries or even in multiple geographies rather than having asynchronized work hours. Otherwise, if clarifications have been sent out via an email, you will receive the email just next day and again, in these clarifications [might be] some things you do not understand [...]." (Interviewee 1, 353-360)

5. Discussion

5.1 Summary of Findings and Implications

Building upon my pre-defined research question, the main goal of this research project was the verification of already identified agile communication practices in a large IT project context and, additionally, the extension of this pool by identifying new communication methods through expert interviews. Based on section 4, I was generally able to give answers to this research question and enhance the knowledge on communication in AGOSD project from both a theoretical as well as practical point of view:

(1) Contribution to research. First, although having conducted a structured literature view on distributed agile outsourced communication practices, I did not find any new methods. Hence, it indicates that the depicted overview (Table 2) is pretty complete.

Second, due to the ranking within the different categories, it is clearly recognizable that there are practices which both interviewees rated with a 5, namely *establishing team member trust, improvement of cooperation, "One Team" – mentality, creation of a joint knowledge base* and *groupware tools*. Thus, the first three practices can be summarized as soft team skills and imply that the inter-organizational respectively inter-team relationship is essential for a productive collaboration. A common knowledge base and knowledge sharing via groupware tools are the enabler for time saving, allocating up-to-date information and reducing redundancy, since documentation is team-wide provided.

Third, I was able to identify an additional dedicated distributed agile communication practice, namely *"Lessons-Learned" - sessions.* It indicates that an examination of a finished sprint regarding pros and cons may improve the next iteration by elevating the ability to work more effectively and bringing down the amount of faults.

(2) Contribution to practice. I contribute to practice by spotlighting the importance of building a harmonized relationship between distributed agile teams. Consequently, team leads should put high effort on aligning the teams' communication, making them to work together and thus, getting rid of silo thinking.

On the technological side, groupware tools are a must-have, so that distributed teams can work as one virtual team effectively and jointly together. Hence, investments in adequate IT infrastructure must not be underestimated since it strongly contributes to a productive collaboration. Taking into account of having backlogs, which is a rationale of Scrum, the current statuses of sprints within the agile project are real-time synchronized and thus, every team member has access to the same information. Furthermore, face-to-face communication tools are supposed to be applied, as they simulate a virtual conversation and thus, people get to know each other better by raising the relationship on a more personal level.

5.2 Limitation and Future Research

With the verification of the known communication practices in AGOSD in large projects the extension of this set and ranking to its practical relevance, I contribute to both theory and practice considering the current research status. Nevertheless, there are some limitations in my study and corresponding research directions that have to be acknowledged.

First, due to time restrictions, I had to take into account that the total number of expert interviews aggregates to two. Consequently, during the evaluation and data consolidation, a precise ranking (each rank is given just once), by computing the mean, was not applicable. As a result, I could not clarify which communication practice is more important than another one (e.g. Table 3, category 5). In addition, the small sample size does not enable to generalize my findings. To encounter these problems, I encourage to increase the sample size, so that a saturation will be leveled off. However, it is important to keep in mind, that the research design is developed within the framework of large IT projects.

Second, the current communication practices, I asked in the interviews for, comprise agile development methods as abstract term, i.e. there is no differentiation between established agile approaches such as Scrum, Kanban, Extreme Programming, Feature Driven Development etc. although each of them has its own specific characteristics. This fact also strengthens the problem of generalizability. Therefore, I suggest that future research endeavors cope in particular with the just mentioned agile practices for gaining significant outcomes and to make them more transparent for practitioners.

6. Conclusion

Within my research endeavour, I was able to make more transparent the practical relevance of current communication practices within AGOSD projects. By applying a qualitative research method, namely expert interviews, I pointed out the importance of communication practices and thus, I was able to deploy a ranking. I am confident, that this paper helps to sensitize the awareness that the inter-team communication within AGOSD projects has a predominant position and is the guidepost for success or failure. Wrapping up, I recommend to conduct further research on specific agile methods as mentioned in my study and extend the sample size for the interviews.

7. References

[1] P. Abrahamsson, J. Warsta, M. T. Siponen and J. Ronkainen, *New directions on agile methods: a comparative analysis, Software Engineering, 2003. Proceedings. 25th International Conference on*, Ieee, 2003, pp. 244-254.

[2] C. Bartelt, M. Broy, C. Herrmann, E. Knauss, M. Kuhrmann, A. Rausch, B. Rumpe and K. Schneider, *Orchestration of Global Software Engineering Projects-Position Paper, 2009 Fourth IEEE International Conference on Global Software Engineering*, IEEE, 2009, pp. 332-337.

[3] M. Buslovic and S. Deribe, "A Multiple Case Study on Contradictions and Pre-conditions for Outsourcing Agile Software Development Projects", (2012).

[4] D. Damian, F. Lanubile and H. L. Oppenheimer, *Addressing the challenges of software industry globalization: the workshop on global software development, Proceedings of the 25th International Conference on Software Engineering*, IEEE Computer Society, 2003, pp. 793-794.

[5] T. Dreesen, R. Linden, C. Meures, N. Schmidt and C. Rosenkranz, *Beyond the Border: A Comparative Literature Review on Communication Practices for Agile Global Outsourced Software Development Projects, 2016 49th Hawaii International Conference on System Sciences (HICSS)*, IEEE, 2016, pp. 4932-4941.

[6] M. Fowler and J. Highsmith, "The agile manifesto", Software Development, 9 (2001), pp. 28-35.

[7] S. Hastie and S. Wojewoda, "Standish Group 2015 Chaos Report-Q&A with Jennifer Lynch", Retrieved, 1 (2015), pp. 2016.

[8] J. Highsmith and A. Cockburn, "Agile software development: The business of innovation", Computer, 34 (2001), pp. 120-127.

[9] H. Holmström, B. Fitzgerald, P. J. Ågerfalk and E. Ó. Conchúir, "Agile practices reduce distance in global software development", Information Systems Management, 23 (2006), pp. 7-18.

[10] C. Koch, C. Jørgensen, M. Olsen and T. Tambo, *We All Know How, Don't We? On the Role of Scrum in IT-Offshoring, International Working Conference on Transfer and Diffusion of IT*, Springer, 2014, pp. 96-112.

[11] M. C. Lacity, S. Khan, A. Yan and L. P. Willcocks, "A review of the IT outsourcing empirical literature and future research directions", Journal of Information technology, 25 (2010), pp. 395-433.

[12] K. C. Laudon, J. P. Laudon and D. Schoder, *Wirtschaftsinformatik: Eine Einführung*, Pearson Deutschland GmbH, 2010.

[13] R. McCauley, "Agile development methods poised to upset status quo", ACM SIGCSE Bulletin, 33 (2001), pp. 14-15.

[14] G. Melnik and F. Maurer, *Direct verbal communication as a catalyst of agile knowledge sharing, Agile Development Conference, 2004*, IEEE, 2004, pp. 21-31.

[15] S. Moore and L. Barnett, "Offshore outsourcing and agile development", Forrester Research, Inc (2004).

[16] M. Paasivaara, S. Durasiewicz and C. Lassenius, *Distributed Agile Development: Using Scrum in a Large Project, 2008 IEEE International Conference on Global Software Engineering*, 2008, pp. 87-95.

[17] M. Paasivaara, S. Durasiewicz and C. Lassenius, *Using scrum in distributed agile development: A multiple case study, 2009 Fourth IEEE International Conference on Global Software Engineering*, IEEE, 2009, pp. 195-204.

[18] S. Sahay, "Global software alliances: the challenge of'standardization'", Scandinavian Journal of Information Systems, 15 (2003), pp. 11.

20

[19] J. Sauer, *Agile practices in offshore outsourcing–an analysis of published experiences*, Proceedings of the 29th information systems research seminar in Scandinavia, IRIS, 2006, pp. 12-15.

[20] N. Schmidt and C. Meures, *" Mind the Gap": An Analysis of Communication in Agile Global Outsourced Software Development Projects, 2016 49th Hawaii International Conference on System Sciences (HICSS)*, IEEE, 2016, pp. 501-510.

[21] P. B. Seddon, S. Cullen and L. P. Willcocks, "Does Domberger's theory of 'The Contracting Organization'explain why organizations outsource IT and the levels of satisfaction achieved?", European Journal of Information Systems, 16 (2007), pp. 237-253.

[22] P. Serrador and J. K. Pinto, "Does Agile work?—A quantitative analysis of agile project success", International Journal of Project Management, 33 (2015), pp. 1040-1051.

[23] I. Sommerville, *Software Engineering. Harlow: Pearson Education Limited, 2007. 824 s*, ISBN 978-0-321-31379-9.

[24] J. Sutherland, G. Schoonheim, E. Rustenburg and M. Rijk, *Fully Distributed Scrum: The Secret Sauce for Hyperproductive Offshored Development Teams, Agile, 2008. AGILE '08. Conference*, 2008, pp. 339-344.

[25] M. Vax and S. Michaud, *Distributed Agile: Growing a Practice Together, Agile, 2008. AGILE '08. Conference*, 2008, pp. 310-314.

[26] J. Webster and R. T. Watson, *Analyzing the past to prepare for the future: Writing a literature review*, JSTOR, 2002, pp. xiii-xxiii.

[27] L. P. Willcocks, S. Cullen and A. Craig, *The Outsourcing Enterprise: From cost management to collaborative innovation*, Palgrave Macmillan, 2010.

[28] V. Yadav, M. Adya, V. Sridhar and D. Nath, "Flexible global software development (GSD): antecedents of success in requirements analysis", Journal of Global Information Management (2009).